Marley the Dreamer

By Nichola Zacher

Marley The Dreamer

Acknowledgements:

Many thanks to everyone on Marley's team who helped me so much.

I'd like to thank Shelley M. Jenkins for her support, love and encouragement with the book.

For Dan and Shelley Ellis who provide Marley with a loving home away from home whenever needed.

Also thank you to Dixie, and my friend Kathy and her sons Joseph and Michael. They share the message of love every day.

I love and appreciate you all.

Thanks to Captivating Covers & Plots for the cover design.

And to all of you, who love and support Marley and look forward to hearing about her next adventures, Marley and I are both so grateful!

Dedication:

To my Father who always showed me unconditional love and supported me in all my achievements. I love you Dad.

Other Book Titles:

Marley dreamed of a life beyond the kettle. She dreamed of having a family who loved her beyond a window. Like every other dog. The small Shorkie wanted to be happy. She wanted to be raised by a loving family. Marley the adorable Shorkie is a mix breed between Shih Tzu and Yorkie. Marley would love to share her story with the world. She wants to tell the world how her new family changed her entire life.

Marley never expected to find love in such an abundance. Finding this caring family was beyond her sleepy thoughts.

Meeting the perfect owners, mommy and grandpa was Marley's first dream to come true.

Marley wants to tell the tale of how she ventures around towns with mommy and grandpa. "Come on in," Marley barks in doggy language as she wags her tail with excitement. She invites each of you into her life and home.

"Please read my story; it's heartwarming" Marley

would say if she could speak.

So, let us venture into Marley's world!

Marley plays with the neighbors. She is not afraid of larger dogs. Marley loves her doggy friends, Bear, Angus and Dottie. Marley likes to show off in front of them. If mommy walks pass Bear's house, Marley yanks and pulls the leash nearly dragging mommy towards the house. Marley then runs around in circles around Bear. She is excited to see him.

But, Marley has one special friend that she has puppy love for, and he is a handsome little fellow. They hope one day they will create a story of their own.

When Nichola received Marley, she was instructed by the trainer to treat Marley as if she was a baby. The trainer warned Nichola that Marley would test the limits. So, she, mommy would have to be firm.

However, just like any parent, never yell at the small Shorkie, nor associate her name with anything bad. Marley loves her mommy with all her doggy heart. Mommy teaches Marley everything.

Marley loves how mommy teaches her how to become a Shorkie with class. Mommy teaches Marley how to have fun and when to set boundaries.

Marley gets overly excited when mommy enters the room. Mommy picks up the small Shorkie because mommy's excited as well. Marley climbs up onto mommy's neck; she then runs around it in circles. Mommy smiles and laughs. She has never seen or experienced anything like that before.

Mommy cradles Marley's small body in her arms.

Marley loves to cuddle; she rests her fury head under mommy's chin. Mommy kisses on the small Shorkie ears and neck. She loves laying on mommy's shoulder.

Mommy plays tag with Marley. They run around the bed or the living room table. Mommy suddenly says, "Stop." Marley stops, her tail wags. Marley runs again and mommy says, "Stop," again. She stops and wags her tail with excitement. Marley is mommy's baby. She goes to the stores with mommy. However, she's afraid. She hides under mommy's car seat. Mommy assures her that there is nothing to be afraid of, she would always keep her safe.

Mommy has no privacy, the little Shorkie follows her into the bathroom. Marley sits on the floor next to mommy.

Marley loves sitting with grandpa in his' favorite chair. She sits in his lap. They watch T.V. together.

Marley is very protective of grandpa. The Shorkie stands between grandpa and anyone who comes too close to him. Grandpa reciprocates the same protection. He hugs small Marley in his arms and keeps her protected from the huge trucks. He then repeats his daughter's words, "I will protect you."

He teaches her to find the right gentleman. Find a mate who treat you with kindness and love.

Marley runs back and forth from grandpa to mommy. It's hard to decide where to go because they love her equally.

Grandpa loves telling stories about Marley. He shares all his memories of how Marley the small Shorkie stole their hearts.

Marley loves getting groomed. Afterwards, she gets dolled up with her purple robin. She turns her head. She puts her happy face in the air. She has just the right amount of doggie confidence. She poses in the photograph. Another one of her favorite things waiting for the photographer to capture the right moment.

Marley is as adorable as those precious black eyes and nose. She stares at the camera; her pose speaks volume. "I am Marley." The adorable, happy Shorkie.

Marley is sophisticated, sassy. She struts as she walks. However, she will test the limits, sometimes. Early morning, Marley barks, "ARRRF" to get her way. She barks and barks until mommy says, "Marley, you will not get your way today." Mommy knows best and even Marley needs discipline, sometimes.

Marley loves the beautiful beaches and watching the small tidal waves. She loves taking a long stroll along the seashore while the wind blows her beautiful soft, silky hair.

Yet, she is cautions. She has that dogie instinct. Although the ocean is beautiful and the water sparkles like a crystal glass. It could be dangerous for a small dog like her. So, she stands back as she watches the waves of the sea toss to and fro.

But before she leaves. Marley looks back one last time. Her unique paw prints are left behind to identify who has been there. An adorable Shorkie, Marley.

Marley runs towards mommy and grandpa. She hops up and down on her short legs. She expresses her excitement how much she appreciates them taking her to the beach.

Marley loves tearing up toilet paper. After a long day on having fun, she peeps above the tub as she bathes. She is always camera ready, "Click." She is a doggie model. Marley is not shy around the camera.

Marley also loves ice cream. Something about vanilla ice cream, makes her lick her dark lips. "Delicious," Marley indicates as she barks. She then takes another lick from the cup.

She drinks from the cup if she is thirsty. Marley likes coffee and sweet potatoes, and she likes a special type of bread with a touch of butter.

"Shh!" Mommy whispers as the small snorkie sleeps peacefully. Because mommy knows that Marley has more dreams to fulfil.

One day Marley would find love beyond her family. She would find a mate and have puppies of her own.

The End!

Thank you for reading all about Marley's adventures.

Marley's story will continue in the next book, which will be coming soon!

About The Author:

Nichola Zacher lives in St. Thomas, Ontario, with her father, Robert, and Marley. Nichola was an early-childhood teacher, but nothing compares to taking care of her father and Marley. It has been this life that inspired Marley's Dream Love.

Nichola and Marley enjoy many adventures together, like running on the beach, going for walks, and playing in the park. Marley loves to go shopping or to the bank to meet new people. Nichola loves to rollerblade and Marley runs beside her. One of Marley's favorite treats is to get a small ice cream cone from McDonald's. Marley also enjoys going to the movies with Nichola and her father where she can snuggle with them.

Because Marley gives everyone she meets lots of love and hope, Nichola wrote Marley's Dream Love to share her with as many people as possible. And since then, the adventures of Marley have continued to blossom!

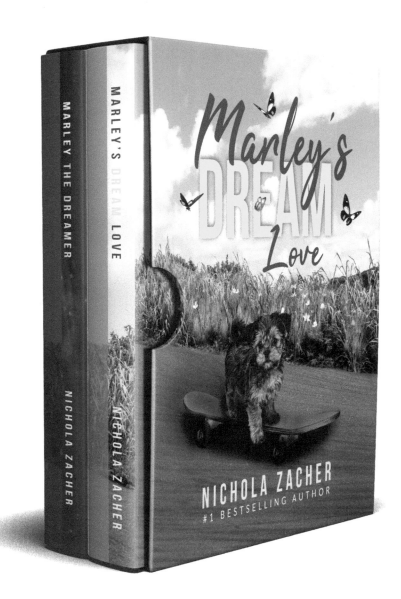

Lightning Source UK Ltd.
Milton Keynes UK
UKHW050329240421
382509UK00002B/56

9 781989 539095